THE WORLD OF AUTOMOBILES

Concept Cars: Past and Future

Written by Norm Geddis

The World of Automobiles

Carmakers from Around the Globe

Concept Cars: Past and Future

Customizing Your Ride

Hop Inside the Most Exotic Cars

Toughest Trucks from the Streets to Showtime

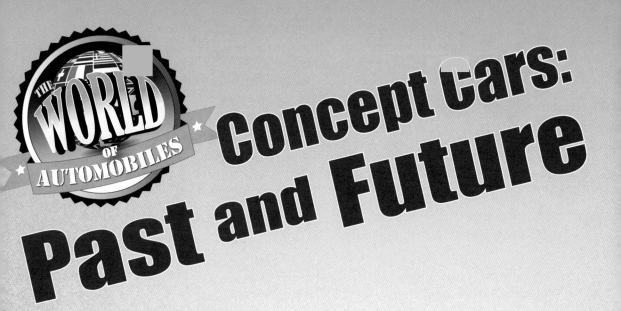

THE WORLD OF AUTOMOBILES

Concept Cars: Past and Future

Written by Norm Geddis

MC

MASON CREST

Mason Crest
450 Parkway Drive, Suite D
Broomall, Pennsylvania 19008
(866) MCP-BOOK (toll free)

First printing
9 8 7 6 5 4 3 2

ISBN (hardback) 978-1-4222-4088-5
ISBN (series) 978-1-4222-4086-1
ISBN (ebook) 978-1-4222-7707-2

Library of Congress Cataloging-in-Publication Data

    Names: Geddis, Norm, author.
    Title: Concept cars : past and future / Norm Geddis.
    Description: Broomall, Pennsylvania : Mason Crest, [2019] | Series: The world
       of automobiles.
    Identifiers: LCCN 2018018046 (print) | LCCN 2018018564 (ebook) | ISBN
       9781422277072 (eBook) | ISBN 9781422240885 (hardback) | ISBN
       9781422240861(series)
    Subjects: LCSH: Experimental automobiles.
    Classification: LCC TL240 (ebook) | LCC TL240 .G43 2019 (print) | DDC
       629.222--dc23
    LC record available at https://lccn.loc.gov/2018018046

Developed and Produced by National Highlights Inc.
Editor: Andrew Luke
Interior and cover design: Annalisa Gumbrecht, Studio Gumbrecht
Production: Michelle Luke

QR CODES AND LINKS TO THIRD-PARTY CONTENT

CONTENTS

KEY ICONS TO LOOK FOR:

Words to understand: These words with their easy-to-understand definitions will increase the reader's understanding of the text while building vocabulary skills.

Sidebars: This boxed material within the main text allows readers to build knowledge, gain insights, explore possibilities, and broaden their perspectives by weaving together additional information to provide realistic and holistic perspectives.

Educational Videos: Readers can view videos by scanning our QR codes, providing them with additional educational content to supplement the text. Examples include news coverage, moments in history, speeches, iconic sports moments and much more!

Text-dependent questions: These questions send the reader back to the text for more careful attention to the evidence presented there.

Research projects: Readers are pointed toward areas of further inquiry connected to each chapter. Suggestions are provided for projects that encourage deeper research and analysis.

Series glossary of key terms: This back-of-the book glossary contains terminology used throughout this series. Words found here increase the reader's ability to read and comprehend higher-level books and articles in this field.

carriage
a word that came over from vehicles pulled by horses and was applied to cars in the early years of automobiles; the word describes a car's body

concept cars
cars created with the intention to inspire new ideas about car design and mechanics, but not to go into production itself

prototype cars
cars created with the intention of getting ideas to refine that same car into a production vehicle

regulations
sets of laws, rules, or other orders prescribed by authority

CHAPTER 1

A Collection of Ideas

Cars have always been about what could be—new places to go, new things to do. Unlike the train, which first opened up travel across continents, cars are not dependent on a schedule of stops and a system of tracks. They can take a traveler anywhere as long as there's a road and even some places where there isn't one.

The tradition of cars being about freedom, the open road, and long-distance travel may come to a pause or an end in the next few decades. Internal guidance systems, artificial intelligence, and self-driving mechanisms are all about to become a part of almost every car. Likely, no matter how fun the design team makes a car with interactive avatars

Some car lovers will miss the smell of gasoline when electric cars take over the market.

and media choices, something will be missing from the experience. Maybe people will miss the smell of gasoline when electric power takes over, or the roar of their engine since electric cars are quieter.

As long as there are people in cars they are going to want a comfortable, safe, and enjoyable ride. Every year carmakers improve the comfort and of the previous year's models. The public expects continual innovation in the function of their cars. Today, car buyers are demanding that car companies improve fuel efficiency and emission controls. A decade into the twentieth century, getting a full **carriage** on a car with a roof was the innovation that got people into interested in buying one.

A lot of rules govern making a car. Safety standards require that front and rear windshields allow for a full view of the road and that all seats have seatbelts. Cars are designed today so the force of an impact is directed away from the cabin as much as possible. These rules limit a car's shape in numerous ways. Engineers form angles and curves in the body in such a way that on impact energy is pushed away from the car. A few decades ago cars were boxier and accidents resulted in more injuries and deaths.

Watch this GM short film from the 1956 Motorama show. The film shows what concepts GM had for future automobiles. The future in this video is 1976.

But why are other things about cars the way they are? Why aren't cars any wider, for example? Aside from engineering hurdles, road width is the main reason cars are only as wide as they are. So why not just make roads wider? There really is no reason for that other than tradition. Roads are as wide as they are because they've pretty much always been around three meters (10 feet) wide. European road lanes are 2.7 meters wide as was dictated by the laws of ancient Rome.

For military, political, and commercial purposes, the ancient Romans began the construction of long straight roads like this one. By law, they were 2.7 meters wide, a tradition that exists to this day.

So, some constraints in making a car come from laws and **regulations**, others come from tradition. Both change over time, but typically in small steps. Car innovations tend to come in big leaps.

A History of Invention

Creating a new car today takes a team of people. Designers, engineers, quality control experts, and legal experts all take part in creating new cars. This wasn't always the case. As with any new technology, it takes decades before problems become apparent and governments make laws in attempts at solutions.

In the early years of car making, there were few rules. Anyone who could build or buy a car could drive it as long as there was a road it could drive on. Where there are few rules, there is a lot of experimentation. Early cars ran on steam and electricity. It wasn't until around 1920 that gasoline-powered cars dominated the market.

Around the same time, the first big auto show took place in New York City. Although it wasn't the first gathering of cars in an auditorium, the 1900 Horseless Carriage Show, sponsored by the Automobile Club of America, has been long considered the first modern auto show. It was a weeklong event held in early November of 1900 at Madison Square Garden. Just about anything that could have wheels was represented at the show. *The New York Times* reported the day after the opening, "There were heavy delivery trucks, delivery wagons, large and small, such as are becoming familiar sights in the streets, cabs, carriages, broughams, and the dozen and one styles of fashionable Victorias, traps, surreys, phaetons, runabouts, and carts."

WHAT A DIFFERENCE A CENTURY MAKES

Ford did not participate in the 1900 auto show at Madison Square Garden. Of all the carmakers that did participate, none remain in operation today. Oldsmobile was the last Horseless Carriage Show carmaker to shutter its doors. The last Olds came off the assembly line April 29, 2004.

What's a brougham, or a Victoria, or a phaeton, or those other weird nouns? These were different types of carriage shapes that were typical of horse-drawn carriages.

Phaeton is the name of a style of horse carriage. Many early vehicle models adopted this name.

Here's where concepts come in. Whenever a new technology becomes popular, companies struggle to understand what makes their product sell better or worse than competitor's similar products. Entrepreneurs try anything they can think of. After a while, the successful companies figure out what people want. In the early days of the Internet, startups threw up anything and everything for sale. Some things sold well on the Internet, others didn't. Companies that figured out what sold and what didn't still are in business today, like Amazon and eBay. Others like eToys and CDNow either folded or were purchased by bigger companies.

Car companies evolved the same way. The concept in the early days was, more or less, to put motors on horse carriages—hence the term horseless carriage. Cars didn't get their own design standard until around 1910 when Ford and Oldsmobile had assembly line production churning out cars with sunken seats, roofs, and the engine in the front.

As some carmakers like Ford and General Motors (GM) grew and grew, others with names like Auburn and Apple (yes, there was a short-lived car company called Apple around 1915) folded or were bought up by the bigger companies. Usually, a big car company would buy a smaller car company because of a new innovation. GM bought Oldsmobile because Ransom Olds, the founder, had developed an assembly line system at least as good as Henry Ford's.

After a couple of decades of gobbling smaller car companies, the large automakers were in a position where they had to

General Motors bought Oldsmobile in large part because founder Ransom Olds had developed an assembly line that rivaled that of Ford's (seen here).

come up with ideas on their own. Throughout the 1920s car companies made a lot of **prototype cars**. These were vehicles that were intended to go into production. The cars were built and road tested. Bugs were resolved. Design plans were refined and eventually the car was sent into production.

Concept cars are something different. They are meant to showcase a range of ideas that could be incorporated into other cars, but these cars themselves are not meant to go into production. Why don't these cars go into production if they're so great? Because the assembly line production of these kinds of cars would be so expensive that the car would have a high price tag and probably wouldn't sell well. Some

Concept cars are meant to showcase a range of ideas that could be incorporated into other cars.

new ideas come together in the lab but cannot be translated to the production line without expensive modification. Sometimes this modification cannot be done because it would interfere with the production of other vehicles.

As an example, power-operated hidden headlamps were part of concept cars from the first concept car, but they didn't become widely available in mid-range sports cars until the 1980s.

A concept car typically will have an innovation in shape or interior comforts. Often, they contain so many ideas that it would be impractical to own and operate one much less make them on an assembly line. Cars like these are meant to wow an audience and inspire engineers. The gadgets and beautiful interior fabrics probably wouldn't stand daily use, especially if owned and operated by a family with young kids.

While the car itself will never go into production, the ideas some of these cars generate last for years, and the cars themselves become legendary. Today there is a lot of interest in car history. However, as late as the 1960s, carmakers were pretty lax about what happened to their concept cars after they had made the rounds of car shows and wowed the audiences.

Some cars became the playthings of the engineers who made them. Others were sent to the scrap heap. One famous concept car languished in a company garage for decades and was thought to be lost. Another one caused a major car company to alter their future design plans after it sank to the bottom of the ocean.

THIS CAR WAS ON FIRE

A certain Bugatti can be said to be half prototype, half concept car. The 1935 Bugatti Aerolithe was a car with 170 horsepower and a body constructed of a unique magnesium alloy. The car was made to demonstrate the higher speed allowed by this light-weight alloy. Although the alloy was heat-protected, the flammability of magnesium made it so other carmakers were unsure of whether or not to adopt it. The Aerolithe was likely stripped for parts for subsequent Bugatti cars. However, their magnesium alloy technology was a precursor of the carbon fiber used for the body construction of some supercars today.

In this century, car companies keep their archives organized, and concept cars usually find their way onto the floor of a company's headquarters, or wind up in a museum.

Car companies today are racing to create new concept cars based on electric or hybrid power, with artificial intelligence that can drive the car itself. A big change is coming in the way people own and drive cars. The ideas that will be a part of cars for decades are emerging now. It's perhaps the most exciting time for car enthusiasts since the earliest days of cars. A lot of technology has come down the line over the last century or so, but nothing as monumentally impactful to what cars are as what's happening today.

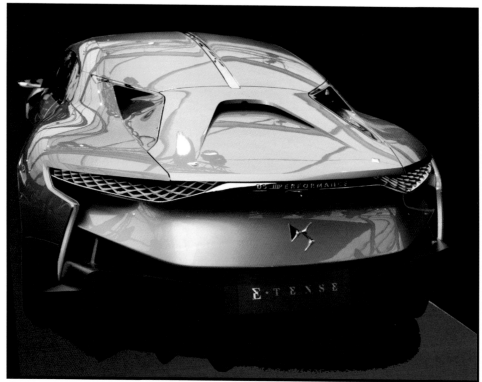

Car companies are racing to create concept cars based on electric or hybrid power, like this E-TENSE Concept Hybrid car from French automaker DS revealed at the International Concept Cars Festival 2017 in Paris, France.

TEXT-DEPENDENT QUESTIONS

1. True or False? Laws and regulations have always played a part in making cars.

2. Why are concept cars not made into production cars?

3. Why are roads always around 3 meters (10ft) in width?

Go to a news website and search for a concept car. At least one will be no more than a few weeks old. Write a report on the most recent concept car you can find. Be as detailed as possible in describing what innovations it has, and all its specifications.

Computer-Aided Design (CAD) – the use of software technology to automate processes that aid in the making, changing, testing or refinement of a design

consultant – one who gives professional advice or services

marketing – the process or technique of promoting, selling, and distributing a product or service

Golf I 1974-1983

CHAPTER 2

Creating a Concept Car

Some car designers are so famous and influential that they get whatever they ask for. When Carroll Shelby, the industry-famous race car driver turned designer of the Cobra and Ford Mustang in the 1960s, went to work for Dodge, he was given free reign to modify Dodge models. If he made a small adjustment to the engine tuning, the car would bear his name. The biggest role he played for Dodge was as a **consultant**. He was instrumental in the design and development of the Dodge Viper.

Carroll Shelby, famous for designing the Ford Mustang, helped to concept the Dodge Viper when he moved to Dodge in the late 1980s. This 2014 version is a 5th generation model.

Raymond Loewy, who designed everything from locomotives to spacecraft, was a consultant for Studebaker, an Indiana-based carmaker that went out of production in the United States in 1963. Two years earlier, his design firm was given the task of a ground-up design for a new Studebaker car that would appeal to young people. The result was the now sought-after Avanti. Today, an original 1963 Studebaker Avanti sells for around $30,000.

The list of famous designers who created famous cars goes on. But not every designer who is or becomes famous is able to demand whatever they want from car companies. These are the people who take the stellar creations and bring them down to earth for mass production so everyone can drive them. Some designers have a foot in both worlds. They create common

Italian designer Giorgetto Giugiaro worked on everything from Lamborghinis to more pedestrian cars like the original Volkswagen Golf.

and exotic cars. One designer who has countless cars, both affordable and expensive, in his design portfolio is Italian Giorgetto Giugiaro. If a car company has a dealership, he probably had a design or two of his sitting in the showroom at one time or another.

Giugiaro won Car Designer of The Century in 1999, as chosen by the Global Automotive Elections Foundation, a group set up to determine several century awards related to automobiles. The nomination list consisted of twenty-five candidates.

CENTURY AWARD WINNERS

The Global Automotive Elections Foundation gave four other century awards along with the one for designer, won by Giorgetto Giugiaro. Here are the other awards and the winners:

1. Car of The Century – Ford Model T
2. Car Engineer of The Century – Ferdinand Porsche (creator of Volkswagen)
3. Car Entrepreneur of The Century – Henry Ford
4. Car Executive of The Century – Ferdinand Piëch (Volkswagen)

Giugiaro probably has the longest and most diverse list of accomplishments of any car designer. While he worked on supercars like the Lamborghini Marco Polo concept car from 1982, he also designed more common models like the Volkswagen Golf and Passat, the AMC Eagle, and the

Engineers use computer-aided design (CAD) systems to create the custom components of concept cars.

Hyundai Sonata. At seventy-nine, he is still working and recently designed a tractor for German maker Deutz-Fahr.

But not every car has a famous designer behind it. These famous names don't work alone; they rely heavily on associate designers. If a single individual ever made cars by themselves (it's hard to believe they ever were), it hasn't been the case for at least the last hundred years.

Many cars evolve out of a company's in-house team. The first part of the process is usually a discussion. Designers and engineers look at the market and competitor vehicles. **Marketing** experts may join the discussion. They will share the results of surveys that asked people what they want in a car. Once an idea is formed around what kind of car to make, then the designers make sketches.

Up to this point, the process of creating a concept car and creating a production car is the same. The difference is where the team can let their imagination go. A concept car doesn't even have to have an engine if its main purpose is to display new body or interior features.

The designers can work within a much freer space. They can incorporate the edgiest stuff into concept cars since these cars are never meant for public consumption, only public ogling. However, the goal of a concept car is to show the car company's cutting-edge credentials and to show-off elements that one day may be incorporated into production cars. Once upon a time, cup holders were the stuff of these dream cars. Today, just about every car has cup holders.

After consulting with engineers (who tend to bring designers down to earth), a final series of sketches is drawn and the process moves to the styling and **CAD** phase.

The styling team converges on a final body shape by making clay models from the sketches. The CAD team begins organizing a virtual set of nuts and bolts for the project. If the concept car under development has a drivetrain and an engine, the car will have around five thousand individual parts, all of which have to be compatible.

The CAD system can be used not only to render a drawing of a car but also to simulate environmental aspects like aerodynamics and glare.

After 3D sketches are rendered and virtual testing takes place, it's time to find the parts. Most carmakers get their parts from suppliers, and any concept car will have common parts throughout its systems. But a concept car will also have custom parts which will have to be lab built.

Check out what's new in concept cars for 2018.

The first CAD system was developed in 1963 at MIT. SKETCHPAD was the first graphical user interface. Users could draw straight and curved lines using a light pen.

Once all the parts are in and tested for function, they are laid out on the assembly floor in a "vehicle confirmation build." Parts are tested again, this time to confirm data from the CAD simulations. Once all the parts are viable, and the concept car will definitely come together, the marketing team begins creating buzz. The car is assembled and shown to the world.

For every concept car that makes it to the auto show floor—like this Jeep CJ 66 at the NAI Auto Show in Detroit in 2017—there are dozens that never get out of the design phase.

The entire project can take about a year, sometimes longer. Often companies will put concept projects on hold when an essential type of work needs to be done. This results in many unfinished projects. For every concept car that has been fully realized, there exist drawers full of drawings and garages full of partially finished bodies. An idea was the beginning of every man-made object, but it's a struggle to bring ideas into the world. They require about as much luck as hard work to become real.

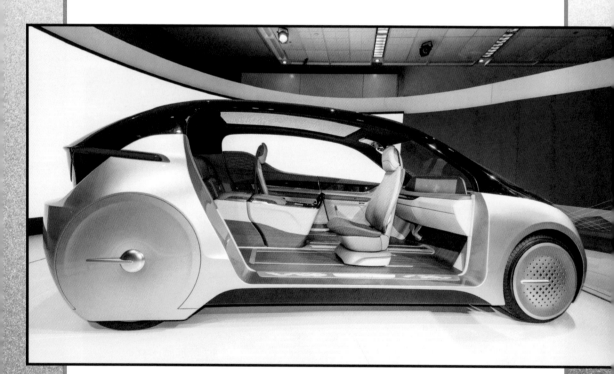

Yanfeng XiM17 Autonomous Concept car Interior at the North American International Auto Show (NAIAS), Detroit, MI – January 12, 2017

TEXT-DEPENDENT QUESTIONS

1. About how many parts will be used in making a fully functional concept car with an engine and drive train?

2. Explain the difference in creating a concept car versus a production car?

3. What is the purpose of a concept car?

 # RESEARCH PROJECT

Free CAD software is available for download. Find and use a simple CAD app. See what kind of car you can come up with.

WORDS TO UNDERSTAND

dream car – another term used for a concept car, since they are made up of designer's dreams

everyman – a term used to describe ordinary working people

Great Depression – a period of disastrously low economic and business activity, beginning in late 1929 with a stock market crash and ending in the late 1930s

Soviet Union – a former communist state made up of today's Russian Federation, Ukraine, Belarus and other now independent states

CHAPTER 3

The History of Concept Cars

By the 1930s, competition among automakers was fierce. **The Great Depression** put the idea of an **everyman** car like the Model T in the backseat. With the unemployment rate hovering around twenty percent, car companies were working on making their automobiles luxurious and were competing for business among the wealthy.

The Great Depression is typically thought of as a time when no one had any money. This isn't true. A great many people were out of work, suffering, and being exploited by the

Inexpensive cars like this 1932 Ford Tudor were still made during the Great Depression, but in fewer numbers as the ordinary people who would buy them could no longer afford to own a car. Carmakers focused on high-end buyers instead.

employers they could find. But it was also true that some people made money during the Depression, those who were taking advantage of the desperation of those who were suffering.

Back in those days, the plight of those suffering was not the car companies' problem. Many car companies took advantage of Depression anxiety and paid lower wages and maintained less clean and safe workplaces. "This is just the way things are" was a common refrain. So, it was with this mindset that car companies first came up with the idea of a concept car.

Chrysler and Ford continued to churn out $500 cars like the Chrysler 6 and Ford Tudor Sedan, but even those two large car companies had far more models starting at twice the price.

The desire to focus on a narrow bandwidth of the potential car-buying market led car companies to seek people who could provide some clairvoyance. No, they didn't hire psychics, but something close. Car companies expanded their marketing divisions and sent armies of marketers into the world asking high-end car buyers what they wanted in an automobile.

The answers led car companies to showcase these cars at established auto shows in major cities. The people who were able to spend $1,000 or more (roughly $20,000 in today's dollars) on an automobile were most sought after by carmakers. This created an event-like nature for the display of new models. Car companies were able to draw in large crowds filled with just the kind of potential customers they were looking for. In this environment, the first concept car was born.

Buick Y-Job

In 1938 Buick put their best ideas into a single car, never intending for mass production of this **dream car**, instead intending to wow the crowd with so many great features packed into one car. The car, the Buick Y-Job, was fully operational, and the designer, Harley Earl, made it his own personal car for thirteen years.

The Y-Job had the first appearance of the trademark Buick bulbous hood and gunsight hood ornament, along with the waterfall grille still in use on Buicks today. The wraparound bumpers and large fenders were two more firsts for Buick, an innovation among all cars from the late 1930s. This was also the first car with hidden, electric operated, headlamps. What made the Y-Job truly revolutionary was the electric operated hardtop. This car was the precursor to the convertible.

After Harley Earl was finished with the Y-Job for his personal use, the car went into storage and was forgotten about until

The 1938 Buick Y-Job has been called the world's first concept car.

The 1938 Phantom Corsair could seat six passengers, with four up front and two in the back.

being rescued in the early 1990s. The car now sits in the GM Design Center as part of their Heritage Collection.

Buick brought some of the stylings of the Y-Job back to life in their 2001 Buick Blackhawk. The car's hardtop, grille, and headlamps all harken back to the world's first concept car.

Phantom Corsair

Now residing as an attraction in Reno, NV, at the National Automobile Museum, the 1938 Phantom Corsair has a tragic story.

The Phantom Corsair was the brainchild of Rust Heinz, heir to the Heinz Ketchup family fortune, a man with no experience making cars. He managed to persuade his aunt to fund his "car of the future" project.

The result was a two-door sedan that was truly ahead of its time; it was so far ahead of its time that it seemed to confuse potential buyers. The interior roof had a range of indicators letting the driver know if a door was ajar, and if the headlamps or radio was left on. The doors opened by an electric push button that could be operated from either the door or the instrument panel. As for comfort, the Phantom Corsair could seat six, four up front and two in the back. Only two passengers could fit in the back because most of the area in the back was taken up by a beverage cabinet. In the front, two of the passengers could sit to the right of the driver and one to the left!

A single Phantom Corsair was completed in order to attract buyers and investors to the new car company. Rust Heinz created a huge marketing campaign, with full-page ads and a World's Fair billboard. Not a single buyer or investor came forward. Eventually, Heinz gave up and drove the car as his personal vehicle. He was killed in a car accident in the summer of 1939. He was not driving the Phantom Corsair. The car stayed in the Heinz family for several decades and then went through a chain of owners, one of which painted it gold. The car was purchased by the Harrah Collection and now sits in a Reno museum.

Dymaxion

Buckminster Fuller was an American architect, designer and inventor who dabbled in a wide variety of fields. He called himself a "comprehensive anticipatory design scientist." One of his many mind-twisting inventions was the Dymaxion, which could be considered the world's first mini-van or recreational vehicle. Three Dymaxions were made in the 1930s, and automakers were interested in many of Fuller's innovations.

Dymaxion designer R. Buckminster Fuller was better known for creating geodesic domes like this one in Montreal completed in 1967.

The car had three wheels with two up front and one in the back. The steering operated the back wheel while the drivetrain handled the front wheels. This allowed the Dymaxion to move in a tight circle, its signature feature. The idea was that this car represented the future and would be a model for an eventual vehicle that would be a car, boat, and plane all in one. The vehicle had a top speed of 115 mph.

In reality, though, the Dymaxion was too much too soon and the number of innovations in the vehicle made it dangerous, resulting in two tragic accidents.

The first happened at the 1933 Chicago World's Fair. The Dymaxion was being driven by race car driver Francis T. Turner at the time when it was hit by another car. The top

See original footage of the Dymaxion in action, including a speeding ticket Buckminster Fuller received while driving it.

caved in killing Turner and injuring his two passengers. One of the passengers injured was British aviation pioneer, and future Japanese spy, William Sempill. Fuller received a concerned call about Sempill's condition from the King of England at the time, George V.

The second accident occurred while Fuller was driving the Dymaxion with his wife and daughter aboard. On the way to a ceremony at Harvard University, the car flipped over. Neither Fuller nor his family was seriously injured, though the accident caused Fuller to rethink the Dymaxion. He too agreed the vehicle was dangerous and too far ahead of its time. He sold off the vehicles and closed his car making business.

Only one Dymaxion survives today, and that one almost didn't make it. In the interest of automotive history, three students from Arizona State University should receive thanks for their keen eyes, and the $3,000 they were able to scrounge together.

Only engineering students would have known what they were looking at. While driving the backroads of Arizona one day they noticed the Dymaxion sitting in the middle of a farm pasture. Upon inspection, they saw it was being used as a chicken coop. They found the farmer who told them he had bought it a decade ago for one dollar. The students bought the Dymaxion after making a generous $3,000 offer. After all, the farmer did not know the importance of the vehicle and the interior was rusted and filled with chicken poop.

The only surviving Dymaxion also now sits in the Harrah Collection at the National Automobile Museum.

The last surviving Dymaxion on display at the National Automobile museum in Reno, NV.

Among Buckminster Fuller's many inventions was the Dymaxion Bathroom, which was itself fitted into one of his vehicles. The Dymaxion Bathroom manages to provide hygienic showers and waste disposal using only a cup of water per person per day.

GAZ-A-Aero (1934)

Though the motivations of the **Soviet Union** were not the same as Buick's, the communist country's state automotive firm may have been the first to create a concept car in 1934.

They wanted to show that their government-run car industry could produce a race car like the United States and free market European countries. The result was the GAZ-A-Aero. Only one was made, and it was constructed of wood with metal plates. The main innovation of the GAZ-A-Aero was the aluminum head which increased compression in the engine. This would have been much more impressive an innovation if the engineers could have gotten it to work with a 6-cylinder engine. They could get the aluminum head to work only with a 4-cylinder engine. This gave the car a top speed of 105 mph, not the kind of speed that would burn up the race tracks in the 1930s. While it may have been the fastest Soviet car made before World War II, it would have never been able to compete with faster European or American race cars. The car never competed in a race.

Alpha Romeo Navajo

What were they thinking? Just to put this contraption into perspective, any kid in the 1980s worth his or her Star Wars toys would have thought this car was lame. Alpha Romeo probably didn't care what any kid thought of their contribution to 1980s car design. They were selling their expensive cars to adults. But kids have a great instinct that tells them when adults just don't get it, and that's what this car screamed back in the 1980s. It was completely uncool.

The 1976 Alfa Romeo Navajo was a high-end concept car with a low end sci-fi look.

It tried to be futuristic, but it ended up looking like the sad design of cars and spaceships used in TV science fiction at the time. Cars, ships, and sci-fi stuff from movies—cool. TV show sci-fi vehicles were definitively junky in the 1980s and kids knew it.

Gone were the Batmobile and the Munster's car, replaced with stock car conversions made on the cheap. The Navajo looked like a failed attempt to combine a DeLorean with the Buck Rogers spaceship from the 1980s TV series. A big rear spoiler isn't enough to fool the public when a company is out of original ideas.

The car did have its fans, however, and some of the sleek styling of its front end made its way into numerous European mid-range sports cars of the late 1980s.

Laura (1982)

Here is another car that looks like it should be on a science fiction TV show. Like the GAZ-Aero, this Soviet concept car was made at home as a side project. Two engineers, Dmitry Parfenov and Gennady Hainov, set out to build a car of their own design. This wasn't an unusual way for engineers to spend their free time. Many other engineers built cars at home too. However, this usually entailed using parts acquired from automotive factories. Parfenov and Hainov were different. Almost every part of the Laura was homemade. It had a top speed of just 106 mph, despite being unusually aerodynamic for a Soviet-era car.

The Soviet leader at the time, Mikhail Gorbachev, took notice of the Laura. He praised the car and it was shown off at several international auto shows as the future of Soviet car design. However, only two were ever built. Political deterioration and the eventual collapse of the Soviet Union kept the Laura from becoming more than just another dream car.

A BRUCE WAYNE PRICE TAG

Just a few years ago, Batmobile creator George Barris sold the original Batmobile for more than 4.5 million dollars. DC Comics owns the rights to the image of the Batmobile. Replica makers pay a license fee to DC for permission to make replica Batmobiles.

The 1955 Lincoln Futura concept car became famous when it was redesigned as the Batmobile for TV in 1966.

Lincoln Futura

The most famous concept car of all time is the Lincoln Futura, mainly because it's the car that became the Batmobile of the 1960s TV series. While the Batmobile metamorphosis is an interesting story, the car had an impact on its own during its days in the early 1950s as a concept car going around to car shows.

The Futura has all the stylings that would become common by the late 1950s. The tailfin styling would become a part of numerous Lincolns and influence the design of competitor tailfins. The grille design found its way into 1960s Fords like the Galaxie.

Toys and model kits of the Futura were in stores long before the car became the Batmobile.

TEXT-DEPENDENT QUESTIONS

1. Where was the last surviving Dymaxion found?
2. What was the primary innovation in the Soviet's GAZ-Aero?
3. True or False? The Laura was a car planned by a Soviet Union committee.

RESEARCH PROJECT

Choose a car you are familiar with and try to find a concept car that influenced it. This is most easily done by looking up concept cars from one to five years prior to the model year of your car. Using an enlarged image of the car, highlight and describe the features that were influenced.

artificial intelligence – the capacity of a computer to perform operations that are like learning and decision making in humans

the Consumer Electronics Show (CES) – a large annual convention showcasing new products and emerging technology

kilowatt hour (kWh) – a kilowatt hour is a unit of measure of energy signifying a steady rate of usage measured over time at a constant rate. This unit is used for car battery power designations

CHAPTER 4

Concept Cars Today

What is a car? That's the question automotive engineers are constantly asking themselves. Does a car need a driver? Can the car market support gasoline alternatives? Do people still want cars designed for long distance travel? Cars will have a different place in daily life just a decade or two from now.

Likely, cars will become smaller and sharing will become more common. The SUV became so common in family homes for a reason that may soon no longer exist. As automated deliveries by drone or driverless vehicles become more common, the need for a large vehicle to bring home large shopping hauls will become less common, although the need to chauffeur the kids and their baseball teammates will persist.

Cars will likely function more to transport people than goods, but shopping, road trips, and all the fun we already associate with cars will surely continue in some form, although there will be less of it. Does that mean everyone becomes a hermit or family of couch potatoes? New and as yet unknown motivations for getting in the car will evolve, but cars may be relevant for different reasons.

Many budget- and environmentally conscious young adults are avoiding purchasing cars, viewing ride- or car-sharing as a better alternative to car ownership. But that isn't keeping car companies from creating cars that will fit into their emerging lifestyles. Some of these cars anticipate new millionaires and billionaires among the millennial generation.

Toyota Concept-i

Toyota's future will be all about you and me and anyone who owns one of their intelligent cars that will, as Toyota puts it, "anticipate people's needs, inspire their imaginations and improve their lives." Those are some impressive goals.

The Concept-i is Toyota's idea of what a car will be like in 2030. This is the direction Toyota is wants for their production cars a dozen years or so from now. The Concept-i has an **artificial intelligence** system tweaked for a personalized user experience that will be, first and foremost, fun.

Toyota doesn't anticipate completely driverless cars by the year 2030, so they've put a game controller type steering wheel front and center. The Concept-i does have a driverless "chauffer mode." The spooky thing about the car is the

The Toyota Concept-i has a driverless chauffeur mode and an artificial intelligence system named Yui that can converse with the driver.

AI system. Perhaps in a decade or so we'll be used to conversing with computers that have a face, of sorts, and talk back to us.

Watch the official unveiling of the Concept-i.

The Concept-i's AI system is called Yui, and it has an animated avatar that can talk to the driver. It can also flit around to various screens in the car on its own. Yui's avatar is a ringed sphere. According to Wired magazine, who spoke with a Toyota representative at 2017's CES, the outer ring represents its body, the inner sphere, its soul. Yui is always watching the driver and the road, and can give warnings or take over control if it determines the driver is distracted or road conditions are hazardous.

Yui can even appear on the car's exterior door panel to greet the driver and say, "hello." Perhaps it also will be able to tell a would-be car thief to, "get lost!" Preventing carjacking-by-hack may be an important duty for Yui too.

Toyota has also made the Concept-i Walk—a Segway type sidewalk scooter that occupies only as much width as a single pedestrian. Yui is also present on the Walk, looking out for unseen objects in the path and being generally friendly and helpful.

Honda NeuV

Honda has also come out with a concept car with AI that anticipates driver needs. Their futuristic vehicle is a little more compact than the Concept-i, but it has some unique features of its own. When not in use, the owner can set the car to ridesharing mode and make some money. The NeuV can network with a ride-sharing service, pickup, and self-drive passengers.

If additional income opportunity isn't an attractive feature, then how about managing electricity? The NeuV is designed to monitor electricity rates and only consume power when prices are low. When prices are high, this car can actually sell power back to the electric company. And if that's not enough, how about sending the owner's grocery list to the store, along with payment, and picking the groceries up on its own? It's been designed to do just that.

NeuV's AI isn't as personal as Yui. Communication is done through a single touchscreen in the center console. It doesn't talk, or have an avatar. What it will do is sense the driver's mood and make recommendations for appropriate music or other media.

One perk of the Honda NeuV is it can go grocery shopping all by itself, including sending the list, payment, and pickup.

Vision Mercedes-Maybach

First prize for making a viable electric supercar will go to Mercedes if the Vision electric Maybach supercar technology goes into production cars. Mercedes must think this car will be special, as they've changed the naming convention for it by putting the model name up front.

After much fanfare, the Vision was unveiled in late August 2017, at the posh Monterey Car Week in Pebble Beach. The car is a long one at twenty feet. Yet, it only seats four and has two up-swinging doors.

Mercedes-Benz created a three-wheel concept car called the Jet Life in 1997. It was a car that no matter how it was impacted, or how much the driver tried, would not fall on its side or flip over.

Under the hood sits four all-electric motors, one for each wheel, each powered by an 80-**kWh** battery. The car can reach a top speed of 155 mph and go from 0 to 60 mph (0 to 97 km/h) in four seconds.

While the Vision doesn't have an AI like the Concept-i or the NeuV, it does have some interesting AI-like features. The car senses body heat and adjusts the temperature accordingly. A sensor detects the color of the driver's clothing and creates a

The Vision Mercedes-Maybach is twenty feet long with four electric motors and a top speed of 155 mph.

complementary color scheme for the interior. The windshield serves as the cars command console. Mere gestures from the driver flip virtual switches and adjust virtual levers.

TEXT-DEPENDENT QUESTIONS

1. What does Yui's body look like?

2. True or False? The Vision Mercedes-Maybach has four electric motors.

3. What is one way the NeuV can generate a revenue stream for its owner?

RESEARCH PROJECT

Make a sketch of your own concept car and then list the features it will have and its power source.

hallowed – highly respected; revered; sacred

open-wheel racing – a racing event in which the standard car has its wheels outside of the car's body

roadster – an automobile with an open body that seats two and has a folding fabric top and often a luggage compartment or rumble seat in the rear

CHAPTER 5

Concept Cars Take to The Track

Auto racing is a sport unlike any other. The car is at least as important as the driver. In football, baseball, and other major sports, TV commercials for the ball maker don't crowd the commercial slots, and the balls themselves aren't covered with promotional stickers and logos. Racing is as much about the car as the driver. In that sense, racing is closer to the fading sport of bullfighting. There was a time when the great bulls as highly regarded as the bullfighter. Both held a **hallowed** significance in the minds of the spectators. In auto racing, instead of a fighter facing off against an animal that will almost certainly die, a driver faces off against both his machine and the other drivers. Design flaws, mechanical

In auto racing, it is not only driver versus driver, but also driver versus machine.

failures, and misjudgment on the part of the driver can put them in peril. The driver must not only navigate the field of drivers on the race track, but also the challenges that the car itself poses.

Major carmakers make their racing team a large part of their promotional efforts. Showing off their prowess in making winning race cars reflects their excellence in the production-car end of their business. Or, at least that's a perception people have of the relationship between racing divisions and production divisions. It certainly is true that having a winning race car gets a carmaker respect among its peers.

In auto racing, whether **open-wheel**, NASCAR, or other forms of racing, a big opportunity for publicity exists for companies that make attention-getting race cars. That's why sometimes concept cars find their way onto racetracks. Here are some concept race cars that got audiences standing and pointing, saying, "What was that!?"

The biggest innovation of the 2012 Nissan Deltawing was its fuel efficiency.

Nissan's Deltawing

This slimmed-down Batmobile took to the track at the 24 Hours of Le Mans race in 2012. Its biggest innovation was its fuel efficiency. The Deltawing uses about half the fuel of a typical race car its size and weight. Nissan entered the car with the mysterious name of Project 56. This gimmick created a lot of buzz even before the Deltawing took to the track.

Originally, the Deltawing had been proposed as race car for IndyCar, the American open-wheel racing circuit. The organization turned down the car as too radical. So, Nissan switched the focus of the car to endurance racing.

CONCEPT COUPE

A coupe version of the Deltawing was made in 2013. This version had better safety features and conformed to more racing standards than its cousin. The first Coupe (chassis #001) went up for sale in November of 2017 at a price of $375,000 and was the only Deltawing expected to be made available to the public.

Ride with race car driver Katherine Legge in a POV video from inside the Deltawing.

Seen here at Nissan World headquarters in Japan before its debut, the Deltawing raced for four years before regulation changes ended its run.

The Deltawing's racing team had a heartbreaking six hours on the track at Le Mans. The car posted the best lap time of the race at 3:45.737. Unfortunately, a collision with an experimental Toyota hybrid put the Nissan entry out of commission.

Driver Satoshi Motoyama worked alone for ninety minutes to get the Deltawing running again. The rules of Le Mans state that after a collision the car must get to the pit on its own steam or be disqualified. Another rule says that only the driver can touch the car when it's on the track.

The entire racing team came over to shout instructions and advice from the sidelines. The steering system had become too mangled for an on-track repair, and that was the end of the Deltawing's premiere at Le Mans.

The Deltawing was repaired and raced numerous times since its premiere, but it never posted a better lap time. New regulations governing vehicles eventually took the Deltawing off the racing circuit for good in 2016.

The BMW V12 LMR, seen here at the BMW Museum in Munich, won its inaugural race at 1999's 24 Hours of Le Mans.

BMW V12 LMR

In the late 1990s, Grand Tourer cars dominated the 24 Hours of Le Mans race. This scenario gave a great boon to carmakers because these GTs were essentially modified production vehicles, like Nissan's R33 GT-R, the Dodge Viper GTS-R, and the Chevy Corvette C5-R. Grand Tourers got a boost not only on the race track but in the showroom as well.

BMW, however, wasn't going to have any of this GT business, and in 1999 entered a radically redesigned race car. Two BMW V12 LMRs were created and entered into the 1999 24 Hours of Le Mans race.

A few other concept cars along with the BMW faced off against the GTs in the 1999 Le Mans race. Both BMWs did extremely well. Late in the race, they were running first and second, with LMR #001 four laps ahead of LMR #002. A stuck throttle caused #001 to crash. No one was hurt, but the car could not continue in the race.

Now the race was more competitive. #002 was only a lap ahead of the next car, a Toyota. The driver of the Toyota had been hanging back, waiting for an opportunity like this. He put his foot down but as he was approaching the BMW a tire blowout sent his Toyota to the sidelines. At that point, no other car could catch up with the BMW V12 LMR. #002 gave BMW their first overall win at Le Mans.

GODFATHER OF THE GT

Carroll Shelby made some the greatest GT cars ever. As a race car driver he won the 1959 24 Hours of Le Mans race driving a car designed by David Brown.

Infiniti Prototype 9

An all-electric race car with a 1940s look turned heads at the 2017 Pebble Beach Concours d'Elegance. Infiniti's new electric racing car shows off the potential of their electric technology that will premiere in the new Nissan Leaf.

Some further engineering will be necessary before this car can compete. With a top speed of 106 mph, it's at the low end of race car capabilities. Plus, its 30-kWh battery will be depleted after about twenty minutes on the track.

Prototype 9 is meant to harken back to Japanese race cars of the 1940s. At the car's unveiling, Infiniti senior vice president of global design Alfonso Albaisa warmed up the audience with a little thought experiment. "What if we found a car, down at the southern tip of Japan, buried deep in a barn, hidden from all eyes for seventy years? What if in this car we found the seed of passion planted during our first Japanese Grand Prix, and the power and artistry of Infiniti today? What would this discovery look like?"

As romantic as that vision sounds, the Prototype 9 might not be enough to help open-wheel racing. The American open-wheel racing circuit is in trouble.

IndyCar needs innovation badly. Attendance is down and, compared to the popular stock car racing circuit NASCAR, open-wheel racing is in a ditch in this country. But it seems that IndyCar wants to take only small steps. The new aerodynamic stylings they allowed for Chevrolets and Hondas have been unimpressive. In their first use in a race, one of the aero kits flew off a car into the stands, injuring a spectator.

BMW concept Z4

The 2017 Pebble Beach Concours d'Elegance shows off many old and new cars and gave a stage to BMW this year to reveal their long-awaited concept car.

BMW is still being tight-lipped about their new concept car. Sure, it has fantastic eye appeal. And while BMW noted that the three air intakes the car sports are indicative of the power in back, they still have not announced what type of engine and what specs will be in the concept Z4.

When it looks like a twenty-first century updated 1930s roadster and is made by BMW, could the final specs be disappointing? Probably not, but that depends on what else gets revealed in the next few years.

The main purpose of the concept Z4 is to solidify BMW's new design strategy, what they call "Powerful Elegance" — embracing curvy, big, and elegant. So, this car is all about the exterior shape and interior features. Since BMW wants to be all about the driver, they have visually obscured the passenger area with a boldly colored leather dashboard that extends up on the passenger side, and boldly colored leather seats. The effect will be to hide the passenger and make the driver of this expensive car stand out.

This Z4 concept sports car from BMW embodies what the company calls its "powerful elegance" design strategy.

TEXT-DEPENDENT QUESTIONS

1. What type of cars dominated the 24 Hours of Le Mans race in the 1990s?

2. True or False? The Infiniti Prototype 9 is gasoline powered.

3. What is the main purpose of the BMW concept Z4?

 # RESEARCH PROJECT

Visit the Pebble Beach Concours d'Elegance website [https://www.pebblebeachconcours.net] and make a list of your five favorite cars from this year's event. Do some research and detail their specs, indicating what features made you choose them.

Pebble Beach Concours d'Elegance 2012.

WORDS TO UNDERSTAND

antennae – the plural of antenna; these were odd-shaped trees or sticks of metal that allowed for reception of analog radio and television waves

space race – a term used for the competition between the United States and the Soviet Union for first-time accomplishments in space exploration in the 1950s and '60s

turnpike – a term used to describe American toll highways, especially in northeastern states

CHAPTER 6

Lost Legends

Some things get lost. Some things get found. While the historical importance of some automobiles might seem obvious today, the practice many decades ago was to throw old stuff away. Make room for the future. Well, that future took longer to get here than anticipated. Many of those around during the moon landings are still waiting for a ticket on a moon-bound rocket. So as a future with flying cars and automated gadgets looked to be further off, interest in the past filled in for the disappointment. Nostalgia became more important than the future.

Do kids play with toy cars anymore? Well, if Matchbox or Hot Wheels collectibles are not stored by the dozen anymore,

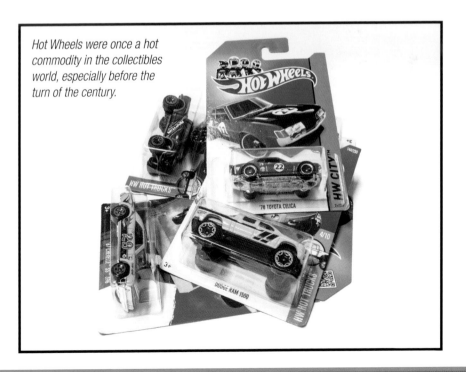

Hot Wheels were once a hot commodity in the collectibles world, especially before the turn of the century.

The fins like the ones on this 1956 Ford Thunderbird were first introduced in the 1955 Ford Mystere concept car.

this experience is still common to several older generations. Small pocket toys like diecast cars got lost a lot. A kid would be carrying them around and playing with them in grass, mud, under leaves. So, losing them was a risk of the game. But then there would be that surprise moment when a car would be re-discovered, usually weathered. But hey, you got something back.

That feeling isn't uncommon to concept car enthusiasts. Remember the Buckminster Fuller Dymaxion discovery on that farm in Arizona? Those students must have felt amazement, satisfaction, and a sense that they had discovered something meaningful.

Some toy cars are worth as much as supercars. In April of 2017, a man brought a Hot Wheels car to an Antiques Roadshow event. His father, a foreman at Mattel, had given the car to him. The Hot Wheels car, a prototype Beach Bomb van, had failed the playtest and been rejected. That meant it had never been mass-produced, and it turned out to be worth $150,000.

Before the later decades of the last century, car companies didn't keep track or really care about their concept cars. Many companies, like GM, let their engineers take their creations home. Sometimes they were junked, used for parts, or otherwise scattered to the wind. Sometimes they were sold or given away, after which they would become the stuff of rumor. As some of these cars passed through many different owners, knowledge of their current status and location became fuzzy. Those who care to keep track of where these cars currently reside like to know if they are still in operation or rotting in a field or garage.

The following are concept cars that have become the stuff of legend, but not necessarily because they were great cars. Some of them like the Norseman could have been revolutionary. But for one reason or another, these cars have disappeared, or are inaccessible in their present location.

1955 Ford Mystere

This car influenced several later model Fords. But that wasn't its claim to fame. The Mystere came with all the pleasures that the 1950s offered in the living room. The car had media galore—a television, radio, and telephone. To accommodate all this media, the car had multiple **antennae**. None of it was real, however. The Mystere was an empty scale model. Ford sought to show all the ideas in design and interior comfort they had in mind for future cars.

As for its body, the Mystere had a glass canopy roof and twin rear exhausts that looked like they came off a jet plane. Its sleek design and low stance made it look like it was floating above the ground.

The phone and television never made it into Ford models, at least not until recent years. However, the side trim and fins became features on some '56 and '57 models.

While the fate of the Mystere is uncertain, an interesting rumor arose on the Internet around 2008. Pictures showed a car much like the Mystere as an advertising gimmick in a restaurant parking lot in Winnipeg.

In an interview, the owner claimed that the car was a modified T-bird. However, the front fenders and other features look distinctly like the Mystere. Some think the owner is confused and his car is a custom job fusing a T-bird with the Mystere.

Watch the Ford Mystere in production and on the auto show floor.

The first car-phone service was a radio frequency-based service that became available in the Chicago area in 1946. The equipment was expensive and bulky. Everyone using the service had to make their calls on three shared channels, which was soon expanded to thirty-two. Services using radio technology existed throughout North America until the 1980s.

1955 Oldsmobile Delta

Sometimes a concept car looks so cool that it seems like a foregone conclusion that it'll end up for sale on a dealer lot. That's not always the case and no one knows for sure what happened to the original Oldsmobile Delta concept car.

The Delta name was applied to versions of the model 88 from the late 1960s onward, but the style was unrelated to the original Delta.

The **space race** of the 1950s put rocket ships at the forefront of everyone's imagination. For many years it seemed as if space travel would eventually work just like air travel. This wild sense of possibility led marketers to associate rocket ships with any product that they could. So, from breakfast cereals to automobiles, designers were working in rocket ship themes any place they could go. Oldsmobile's Delta was their contribution to space age design. The car featured dual fuel tanks in the rear fenders, cast-aluminum wheels, anodized aluminum trim, a center console for radio controls, blue-tinted glass and two-tone metallic blue paint.

1956 Chevrolet Corvette Impala

Yes, at one time the Corvette and Impala were one car—but just one car, one time. Opposite the Olds Delta sat the Chevrolet Corvette Impala, its design rejecting the atomic, space-age looks becoming so popular in the mid-1950s.

Much of the styling on the Corvette Impala would be used on future production Impalas, like the roofline and side trim. The car also incorporated corvette elements, like the grille and grille surround. The hardtop, five-passenger sports sedan debuted at the 1956 Motorama show at the Waldorf Astoria in New York.

Some believe this down-to-earth car was crushed after it made its tour around to car shows. But that doesn't keep others from still looking for it.

Chevrolet's short-lived Corvette Impala debuted at an auto show at the famous Waldorf Astoria hotel in New York in 1956.

1956 Mercury XM-Turnpike Cruiser

Here was another concept car that had a lot of excess. The most excessive thing about the car was its roof. The car had a metal roof that could slide back to expose glass windows that flipped up. Combined with its huge tail lights and its four exhaust pipes, the car looks like something Elvis would be driving through Memphis with a space alien in the passenger seat.

A version of the Turnpike Cruiser went into production, absent the roof system and with toned down features. Even the production version is rare, as the Turnpike Cruiser was a favorite of 1970s demolition derby circuit. So, most of them got smashed up on dirt race tracks.

The concept version is rumored to exist in a well-known collector's garage waiting for a restoration and a surprise unveiling sometime in the next few years.

1956 Chrysler Norseman

A legendary car seen, touched, and driven by almost no one, the Norseman was to be Chrysler's showpiece at car shows throughout the United States and Canada. Chrysler took this car seriously. The Norseman was to be a fully working prototype. It was also, according to Chrysler executives, going to be, "the most automated car in the world."

The styling of the Norseman was set to define Chrysler's look, at least through the rest of the 1950s. The car was so important that Chrysler hired Italian specialty carmaker Carrozzeria Ghia to build the Norseman according to Chrysler's design plans. The automobile Ghia created is known from only a handful of photographs, and its one and only drive went a distance of about ten feet from the garage into its shipping container.

Ghia was a few days late in shipping the Norseman so its carrier to the United States had to be changed at the last minute. The next available ship leaving Italy was a passenger liner, the SS Andrea Doria. This proved to be a fateful voyage, as the Andrea Doria collided with another passenger ship in thick fog on July 25, 1956, sinking to the seafloor off the coast of Massachusetts.

While the Andrea Doria sits two hundred feet below sea level (numerous dive teams have been to the wreck), the placement of ship on the ocean floor makes retrieval of any large piece of cargo an extremely dangerous undertaking. The car would be heavily deteriorated by ocean salt water and little could be learned that isn't already known about the Norseman, except maybe the color, and only if any paint residue survives. That's one of the mysteries of the Norseman. What color was it? While the car was ordered in a dark green, with a light grey interior, the handful of reporters who saw the car noted its color as blue and its interior as red.

In 1956, the passenger liner Andrea Doria sank after a collision with a Swedish ship, with the 1956 Chrysler Norseman concept car in its cargo hold.

While the streamlined, low-to-the-ground look of the Norseman would become a common profile for Chryslers up into the early 1970s, this one-off had some features that should have, but never did, become a standard part of the Chrysler line.

1956 Oldsmobile Golden Rocket

Ready for blastoff? The Golden Rocket took the whole space concept seriously. The extended center nose and recessed side noses make this car look like it's about to crash into the MST3K Satellite of Love.

The headlights were further recessed behind the three-point nose in the interior next to the side noses. The center grille gave the car its threatening forward look, as if it was ready to blow another car off the road.

The Golden Rocket was sort of an unfinished or mutating project. Several modifications were done while it was touring in auto shows. The rear, center fin was replaced at some point with two side fins.

Even the operation of jet planes influenced this car. Front center vents produced an air stream that exited the rear pointed fenders. This was a unique path to producing good air flow.

The innovation that is seen in cars today was the steering wheel command console. This was the first car to put control buttons and switches at the center of the steering wheel.

The car got a lot of attention and press at 1956 auto shows. Official GM policy was to box up concept cars after they had completed their tour. This was said to be for liability reasons. Then there are the frequent discoveries of these cars that are then traced back to GM executives. Some have been found dismantled in former employees' garages. There even exists a rumor that GM buried hundreds of concept cars in the Arizona desert. Aside from that, rumors abound among older people in and around Detroit of sightings of many odd cars on the road in the '50s and '60s.

What happened to the Golden Rocket is unknown, but that doesn't keep people from looking for it.

The future and the past are forever tied together with automobiles. It's as if each time cars progress into the future with new technology and features, the more we miss the way cars used to be, even if it was before any of us were born. In the last decade, the world has seen the last people pass away who were alive before the horseless carriage first went down a cobbled street with no steed in sight.

Technology is beginning to overwhelm cars. Today, the entertainment consoles we have access to in cars are thought to be contributing to accidents. They certainly provide a lot of choices and many of the operating systems lack an easy pathway to get around. Still, are drivers willing to give up countless choices of entertainment in their vehicles? Almost certainly not, which is why AI will be so important in the future. Won't it be easier to ask Yui to play our favorite song than to page through the car's interface while trying to keep an eye on the road?

But Yui and his soon-to-be-birthed cousins look like they will come with a trade-off. Drivers in the future won't have

Entertainment technology in cars today can be overwhelming and difficult to navigate.

immediate access to the freedom cars still hint at and provide today. The default position of the car will be for Yui to pop up and say hello. Drivers will have to make a choice to turn everything off in order to enjoy a quiet ride and complete control of the car's systems. And that's about as likely as being able to stop binge watching a favorite show the day it is released. With all that entertainment, can anyone say no?

Well, at least the retro looks will come around every now and again. The future can sometimes be a bore.

TEXT-DEPENDENT QUESTIONS

1. True or False? The Ford Mystere was found in someone's garage in New Jersey.

2. The Mercury Turnpike was popular for what type of motorsport?

3. What was GM's official policy on what do with concept cars after they had been on tour?

RESEARCH PROJECT

Using the Internet, see if you can identify the second oldest concept car known to exist today (hint: the Buick Y-Job is the first).

Series Glossary of Terms

Aerodynamic Drag

Drag produced by a moving object as it displaces the air in its path. Aerodynamic drag is a force usually measured in pounds; it increases in proportion to the object's frontal area, its drag coefficient, and the square of its speed.

Ball Joint

A flexible joint consisting of a ball in a socket, used primarily in front suspensions because it can accommodate a wide range of angular motion.

Camshaft

A shaft fitted with several cams, whose lobes push on valve lifters to convert rotary motion into linear motion. One or more camshafts regulate the opening and closing of the valves in all piston engines.

Carbon Fiber

Threadlike strands of pure carbon that are extremely strong in tension (that is, when pulled) and are reasonably flexible. Carbon fiber can be bound in a matrix of plastic resin by heat, vacuum, or pressure to form a composite that is strong and light—and very expensive.

Chassis

A general term that refers to all of the mechanical parts of a car attached to a structural frame. In cars with unitized construction, the chassis comprises everything but the body of the car.

Cylinder

The round, straight-sided cavity in which the pistons move up and down. Typically made of cast iron and formed as a part of the block.

Differential

A special gearbox designed so that the torque fed into it is split and delivered to two outputs that can turn at different speeds. Differentials within axles are designed to split torque evenly; however, when used between the front and rear axles in four-wheel-drive systems (a center differential), they can be designed to apportion torque unevenly.

Drivetrain

All of a car's components that create power and transmit it to the wheels; i.e. the engine, the transmission, the differential(s), the hubs, and any interconnecting shafts.

Fuel Injection

Any system that meters fuel to an engine by measuring its needs and then regulating the fuel flow, by electronic or mechanical means, through a pump and injectors. Throttle-body injection locates the injector(s) centrally in the throttle-body housing, while port injection allocates at least one injector for each cylinder near its intake port.

Horsepower

The common unit of measurement of an engine's power. One horsepower equals 550 foot-pounds per second, the power needed to lift 550 pounds one foot off the ground in one second: or one pound 550 feet up in the same time.

Intake Manifold

The network of passages that direct air or air-fuel mixture from the throttle body to the intake ports in the cylinder head. The flow typically proceeds from the throttle body into a chamber called the plenum, which in turn feeds individual tubes, called runners, leading to each intake port. Engine breathing is enhanced if the intake manifold is configured to optimize the pressure pulses in the intake system.

Overdrive

Any gearset in which the output shaft turns faster than the input shaft. Overdrive gears are used in most modern transmissions because they reduce engine rpm and improve fuel economy.

Overhead Cam

The type of valvetrain arrangement in which the engine's camshaft(s) is in its cylinder head(s). When the camshaft(s) is placed close to the valves, the valvetrain components can be stiffer and lighter, allowing the valves to open and close more rapidly and the engine to run at higher rpm. In a single-overhead-cam (SOHC) layout, one camshaft actuates all of the valves in a cylinder head. In a double-overhead-camshaft (DOHC) layout, one camshaft actuates the intake valves, and one camshaft operates the exhaust valves.

Powertrain

An engine and transmission combination.

Rack-and-Pinion

A steering mechanism that consists of a gear in mesh with a toothed bar, called a ""rack."" The ends of the rack are linked to the steered wheels with tie rods. When the steering shaft rotates the gear, it moves the rack from side to side: turning the wheels.

Sedan

As used by *Car and Driver*, the term "sedan" refers to a fixed-roof car with at least four doors or any fixed-roof two-door car with at least 33 cubic feet of rear interior volume, according to measurements based on SAE standard J1100.

Shock Absorber

A device that converts motion into heat, usually by forcing oil through small internal passages in a tubular housing. Used primarily to dampen suspension oscillations, shock absorbers respond to motion.

Spoiler

An aerodynamic device that changes the direction of airflow in order to reduce lift or aerodynamic drag and/or improve engine cooling.

Supercharger

An air compressor used to force more air into an engine than it can inhale on its own. The term is frequently applied only to mechanically driven compressors, but it actually encompasses all varieties of compressors.

Turbocharger

A supercharger powered by an exhaust-driven turbine. Turbochargers always use centrifugal-flow compressors, which operate efficiently at the high rotational speeds produced by the exhaust turbine.

Source: caranddriver.com

FURTHER READING

Dixon, Leon. *Creative Industries of Detroit: The Untold Story of Detroit's Secret Concept Car Builder*. Forest Lake: CarTech, 2017.

Temple, David. Motorama: *GM's Legendary Show & Concept Cars*. Forest Lake: CarTech, 2015.

Stroud, Jon. *Concept Cars*. New York City: Sterling, 2013.

Dredge, Richard. *THE WORLD'S WORST CONCEPT CARS: From Creative Failures to Breathtakingly Ugly Disasters*. New York City: Metro Book, 2010.

EDUCATIONAL VIDEOS:

Chapter 1:
http://x-qr.net/1FkW

Chapter 2:
http://x-qr.net/1Emw

Chapter 3:
http://x-qr.net/1Cyr

Chapter 4:
http://x-qr.net/1HA2

Chapter 5:
http://x-qr.net/1HqM

Chapter 6:
http://x-qr.net/1GZW

INTERNET RESOURCES

http://www.bfi.org/ – Website of the Buckminster Fuller Institute. Has more info on the Dymaxion Car as well as Buckminster Fuller's other inventions and his writings.

http://www.conceptcarz.com/ – Database for concept car information. There are articles and a lot of pictures on thousands of concept cars.

http://www.seriouswheels.com/ – Website focusing on photography of classic and collector automobiles.

http://www.oldcarsweekly.com/ – General website about older cars that has some information on concept cars. The main attraction is the classifieds that have both for sale and wanted ads.

http://www.classicdriver.com/ – A general website about everything drivable, and watches. More or less a site to gawk at one of a kind, and expensive, cool stuff.

http://oldconceptcars.com/ – A blog dedicated to concept cars from the past.

PHOTO CREDITS:

INDEX

INDEX

INDEX

AUTHOR'S BIOGRAPHY

Norm Geddis lives in Southern California where he works as a writer, video editor, and collectibles expert. He once spent two years cataloging and appraising over one million old movie props. He is currently restoring film and video content from the 1950's DuMont Television Network for the Days of DuMont channel on Roku.